C000203244

Write to I

*How tried and tested journalistic
techniques can improve your writing*

Tim Richardson

Meon Valley Press

ACKNOWLEDGEMENTS

I would like to thank Cathy Verghese, Peter Moore and Alli O'Neill for their comments and guidance. Their knowledge regarding language and writing from the worlds of education and business was invaluable.

My thanks go to Joe for his help with all things computer-related – especially graphics – and to Sam, for his insight, support and motivation.

But I have to reserve my kindest words for Helena Gomm, the editor who made this possible. Without her expertise, input and belief, this project would never have made it into print. Thank you.

ISBN: 1511465689
ISBN-13: 978-1511465687

Illustrations by John Plumb
Meon Valley Press
meonvalleypress@gmail.com

To Julia

CONTENTS

Introduction

Whenever anyone asks me for help with their writing, I always ask them the same six-word question: *What are you trying to say?* Six words. That's all. Six words that any child would understand. And yet, together they pose a question that is fundamental to anyone who wants to write effectively. And when I talk about 'writing', I don't mean embarking on some great literary quest of epic proportions. Instead, it could be anything – an email or letter, a report, an article for a newsletter, a case study, a press release, a blog entry, a caption for a poster, a tweet – you name it. Whatever it is you have to write, the first question you have to ask yourself is: *What am I trying to say?* Because if you can't answer that question, how can you possibly begin?

That's what this book is about. It's about helping you find a way to answer this fundamental question – a question that lies at the starting point of any written task. And the best way that I know is based on the tried and tested journalistic techniques that every cub reporter learns at the beginning of their training. These techniques teach journalists how to write the news – whether it's a report from a local village fete or a write-up of a local council meeting. They are the same techniques that are splashed across the front pages of newspapers as they bring us news of events from around the world. While developed for the world of journalism, these techniques are not – and should not be – the sole preserve of the journalistic profession. Far from it!

I believe everyone who has to write should possess these skills. Why? Because at their heart they teach you to write – not just for yourself but, most importantly, for your reader. They teach you to put your audience first. And they give you the tools necessary to lay out information and ideas in a logical and clear way that is easy for your reader to understand. After all, what is the point of writing something if it is not going to be read? Best of all, these skills are transferable to any area of work – PR, marketing, communications, HR, customer service, IT, engineering, health, education – you name it. And once acquired, they will stick with you for life. Not only will the quality of your writing improve, you will also be able to write *faster*. Or in business-speak, it will improve your skill-set and personal productivity.

About this book

Write to be read! is a practical guide which shows you that you don't have to be a journalist to write like one. At its heart is a technique called 'news writing', which teaches you about structure, angle and a disciplined approach to writing that ensures that you get your message across.

This book is aimed at anyone who wants to improve their writing skills as part of their personal or professional development. It is just as applicable to students and school leavers as it is to someone who already has an established career. It is also useful to non-native speakers of English, particularly those who need to write in English for their jobs and who wish to learn how to improve their style and to target their writing more effectively.

The early chapters provide an introduction to news writing and the reasons why it is such an important technique to learn. And it is here that the process and theory of news writing is explained step-by-step. You will quickly begin to understand how identifying key elements can help you find what's relevant and what's not. The news writing technique is followed by an introduction to the 'drop intro' – a device often used by feature writers, which acts as a counterweight to news writing.

Once this has been covered, we move away from the theory and look at examples of how these journalistic techniques can be adapted for use in letters, emails, blogs, memos, etc. Crucially, this book shows how these journalistic techniques can be applied to any written task in the workplace.

Ultimately, it promotes the idea that news writing is a skill that should not be restricted to the newsroom. Instead, it is a discipline that can be learnt by anyone who wants to write well.

Tim Richardson

1 Hold the front page!

There's a buzz of activity in a London newsroom as the final deadline for the day ticks ever closer. A dozen or so journalists are just finishing their copy before submitting it for editorial scrutiny. By now, the front page is confirmed, with the lead story focusing on an explosive celebrity libel case at the High Court in London. The main picture story is the arrival of a pair of tiger cubs at Edinburgh Zoo. And at the bottom, there's a story focusing on the lunchtime eating habits of office workers.

For the editorial staff at *The Daily Grind*, it's almost the end of another busy shift. That is until news emerges of another outbreak of a deadly fish disease that is spreading across the country. Details of the latest incident are still sketchy, but the news is further confirmation that the disease – which could devastate fish stocks – is still on the move. The government is so concerned about the environmental impact that it's calling an urgent meeting to discuss the matter.

'I want that fishy story on the front page!' editor Jeremy Carter shouts across the newsroom as he heads towards his office. 'We'll look like right mugs if we run with that celeb story now when all of this is kicking off. Get a bloody move on!' And with that, he slams his office door shut.

Reporter Danny Green has less than half an hour to write 450 words to meet the tight deadline. Using the press release issued by the Environment Agency – together with his existing knowledge of the story – he gets to work; his sole focus is on getting the story done in time. While he writes, the sub-editor is busy chopping and changing the other front-page stories to make space for the new splash.

The next day, *The Daily Grind's* main headline reads ***Killer fish disease spreads as ministers hold crisis talks***. The paper's main rival leads with ***Grrrr! Cute cubs born at Scottish zoo***.

This is a scenario played out in newsrooms around the world. The changing pace of events, and the desire to be first with the news, means that journalists have to be on their toes, ready to write or rewrite something at the drop of a hat. It's a skill that journalists acquire and develop throughout their careers. But it's also a skill that is transferable to anyone who wants to improve their writing.

News writing

One of the main techniques used by journalists is called 'news writing'. This allows you to get to the heart of a story and shape it in a particular way. It is methodical, structured and disciplined and it allows you to express yourself concisely and with clarity. And yet, it can also be a springboard for great creativity.

News writing isn't just a style of writing or a template or a particular technique that can only be used by journalists. It is also a thought process that can be learnt by anyone. It teaches you to think in a certain style and allows you to tackle problems in a particular way. Once embedded, it will allow you to approach any subject at all and create something worth reading – you'll never suffer from writer's block again.

News writing allows you to interrogate a story, understand it and analyse it before finally figuring out exactly what you want to say. Whether you're a teacher, doctor, architect, PA, manager, administrator or engineer – whatever your job – learning these skills can help improve your writing. After all, being able to write well should be the goal of anyone who is interested in his or her own personal development. And not only will it enable you to improve your writing, you will write more quickly too.

That's why reporter Danny Green managed to bash out the 450-word front-page lead in less than half an hour. It wasn't because he has 'a flair for writing' or because he is 'good with words'. It was because he was trained in news writing.

So, what is news writing?

In essence, news writing is about grabbing the reader's attention and saying everything you want to say up front in the first sentence or two. It is about distilling what you want to say into 20 or 30 words. Some people describe it as putting the conclusion at the beginning of the story, or putting the most important information first, but I think that's too simplistic. News writing is more than that. It's about clarity. It's about brevity. But it's also about untangling a story and putting information into a logical order. Above all, if you employ a news writing approach, it means you're thinking about the most important people in the world – your readers.

There's no easy way to put this, so I'm just going to come out and say it. Writing isn't about you. It's about your readers. Sorry. The idea of the solitary writer working slavishly to give birth to their creation may be romantic, but it has little legitimacy in the workplace. Think about it – what's more important? The process of writing that blog, that case study, that product description … or someone actually reading it and acting on what they've read?

The problem is that from a young age, we've been conditioned to write for ourselves, not for others. We've been encouraged to develop our own 'voice' and to write about ideas, beliefs and fact-based opinions. We've been told how, through a mixture of good grammar and responsible research, we can make arguments in favour of or against this or that. Which is perfect for academia, but not necessarily ideal for the world of work. Let me go further. When you are in education – be it school, college or university – you are guaranteed at least one reader: your teacher, tutor or lecturer. As your educators, they have to read your written work, regardless of the quality of the writing.

And yet, the moment you step into the world of work, you're on your own. You have to fight for your readership. You may have agonised over your CV and covering letter, but that doesn't mean that a potential employer will read it. Just because you've spent two weeks putting together a bid proposal for a multi-million pound contract doesn't mean your potential client has to read every last word. And even a succession of late nights in the office finishing a sales report doesn't guarantee that the chief exec will read it from top to toe.

That's why you have to do everything you can to attract and engage your readership. That's why you have to earn the right to be read.

Curiously, a news story has its own distinct shape. If you were asked to draw the structure of one, it would be an inverted triangle separated by a series of horizontal lines to represent paragraphs.

Why an inverted triangle? That's because the most important information is contained in the top segment, or *paragraph* as it's known. And as you make your way through the story, the information – although all relevant – becomes less and less important. In other words, it's a hierarchical way of writing, where the information decreases in importance throughout the story.

The beauty of this approach is that even if people only read the first paragraph or two, they should – if it has been written in a true news writing style – 'get' the story. Clearly, the more they read, the more they will learn. But if they don't, no matter, because they will have 'got' it from the opening paragraph. After all, in this increasingly busy world of ours, sometimes all we need is the headline information.

Tradition

This tried and tested technique has its roots firmly planted in the traditions of the newspaper industry. Let me explain. When *The Daily Grind*'s editor said he wanted the killer fish disease story on his front page, his staff knew that it was in addition to the other stories. This wasn't a problem for his online team, who publish on the web. They could simply add the new story at the top of their homepage once it was ready. In the digital world, space isn't an issue. However, *The Daily Grind*'s paper editor was hamstrung by the physical lack of space in the newspaper. He could have dropped one of the front-page stories or pulled another from elsewhere in the newspaper. But that would have meant a lot of rejigging and, with the deadline looming, it simply wasn't possible.

However, thanks to the fact that his journalists had written their stories in the news style, he could include them all without rewriting them. How? By simply cutting each story to make space. Since they've been written in the news style, it doesn't matter where you cut the stories because whatever you cut, the rest will stand up by itself.

Whether you read the first paragraph or the first three, the outcome is the same.

A story written in the news style has its own freestanding structure. Written any other way, the story would have to be completely rewritten or pulled apart and stitched back together again. And that takes time – something that is sadly lacking when deadlines are tight. So, the news style approach helps you cut existing stories to fit. But it also provides the framework to write quickly and concisely.

The benefits for the writer

As a writer, using the news writing approach increases your chance of being read. By summing up what you want to say within a paragraph or two, you can be sure that even if your readers only skim the first couple of paragraphs, they will 'get' the information. And if there is limited space, you know you can cut some of the words without having to rewrite your copy entirely.

The benefits for the reader

As readers, we are constantly being bombarded with information. Our time is precious and we don't always want to have to read reams of text when the information could be put clearly and concisely in a paragraph or two. Worse still, we don't want to wade through lots of information to try to figure out the message, idea or concept being put forward. Something written using the news writing technique means that this work has already been done.

The digital divide

If you still don't believe in the virtues of news writing, I have another point to make. Earlier, I said that with online publishing – and that includes anything digital, everything from emails and blogs to e-reports – space isn't a problem. And that's true. Without the physical limitations of paper, space *is* no longer an issue. But that doesn't give writers free rein to ignore wordcounts, because getting people to read what you've written remains a problem. In fact, I would go so far as to say that there is nothing more competitive – nothing more challenging – than getting people to read what you have written. In truth, it's never been harder. Not only are there newspapers, books and blogs, there are tweets, social networking posts and emails and ... well, you get the message. The web has been responsible for an explosion in self-publishing, the like of which has never been seen before. Before the internet, there were newspapers and magazines backed by an army of staff whose job it was to get copy and pictures into print and then physically delivered to readers. Today, anyone can publish their thoughts and ideas and be read anywhere in the world.

With so much competition for readers, writers – and by that, I mean anyone who writes – have to do everything they can to attract the attention of their readers and hold it. News writing does this because it distils the story, the message, the idea or thought and delivers it as a perfectly preserved neat little digestible packet. After all, what's the point of spending hours of your time writing something if no one is ever going to read it? News writing – when done well – is a gift to readers. And they will thank you for it.

Think about it

1 Consider some of the things you've read recently – be they articles, blogs or work-related material. Which did you enjoy reading and what did you find

most useful? Is there a difference in the writing you read for pleasure and that you read for information? Is it possible to have something that is both enjoyable to read and informative?

2 If you failed to read something from beginning to end, why do you think that was?

3 As a reader, think about what you read for pleasure – such as books or magazines – and what you read because you have to. Do you read these things differently and if so, can you work out why?

2 News writing deconstructed

At first, getting to grips with news writing can seem a bit like trying to juggle six balls when you can barely catch one. It can be tricky to begin with, with words and phrases popping out all over the place. But once you start to practise, things will start to fall into place and become easier.

To write in the news style you need to memorise six words. Together, they will help you analyse and assess any story so you can work out what's important and what's not. These six words are: *who*, *what*, *why*, *where*, *when* and *how* (WWWWWH).

Who: Who is this story about? Who are the people that we need to focus on? The 'who' can refer to things and objects as well as people. For instance, it could be a company, a retailer, an event, a gadget, a government department, a local authority or a charity, as well as a person. The important thing to remember is that 'who' refers to the main subject of the story.

What: What is the story about? What has happened? What is happening? What is about to happen? They're simple questions but sometimes answering them can be really tricky. To make matters worse, sometimes there is more than one 'what', depending on how you prioritise things.

Why: Why is this story important? Why is it happening? Why is it interesting?

Where: Where is it taking place? Nearby? In the next town? Overseas? On the moon?

When: When is it taking place? Today? Tomorrow? Next week? Or has it already happened?

Most people are content with just using WWWWW, but sometimes it is good to use *how* as well.

How: How is it – whatever 'it' is – happening? Sometimes, getting this right can be tricky. In fact, it may be that whatever you're about to write about has no *how*. That's fine; not every story has to have a *how*.

Having this list of words – WWWWWH – to hand provides a framework to enable you to decide on the most important information. Together, they will help you get to the root of any story. Handily, they are also the elements that make up the news introduction or intro. For reasons we will discuss elsewhere, your intro is arguably the most important thing you will write. Get it right and the rest will follow.

The easiest way to see WWWWWH in action is to apply it to an actual intro. Here is the background to a story, which will later have the headline *Say 'cheers!' to new plastic wine bottles*:

- A UK-based chain of shops called The Green Wine Co-Op has decided to sell a range of its wines in plastic bottles instead of glass ones.
- As part of the project, The Green Wine Co-Op has been working in partnership with a US firm that specialises in the distribution of liquid goods. The reason behind the move is that plastic bottles are cheaper and more eco-friendly to produce than glass ones, and the lighter bottles are cheaper to transport. Once used, the plastic wine bottles are cheaper and easier to recycle. This means that over the lifetime of the product, using plastic instead of glass helps cut carbon emissions.
- The company is keen to point out that these plastic bottles do not alter the taste of the wine.

By using WWWWWH methodically, we can start to build our news style intro:

Who: Who is this story about? Note that the 'who' here isn't a person but a 'thing', in this case a retailer.
The Green Wine Co-Op

What: What is the story about? What is important?
Introducing plastic wine bottles

Why: Why is this story important? Why is it happening?
To cut carbon emissions

Where: Where is it taking place?
The UK

When: When is it taking place?
Now

How: How is it happening?
By teaming up with a US company that specialises in liquid distribution

Now that we have our information, it's time to start putting it all together. In this case, each element is being added one at a time. But as you can see, there is no specific order we need to follow; indeed, as it becomes more complex it may be necessary to change the order of the WWWWWH so that it makes sense.

The Green Wine Co-Op (**Who**)

The Green Wine Co-Op has launched a plastic wine bottle. (**Who, what**)

The Green Wine Co-Op has launched a plastic wine bottle which it claims could help cut its carbon footprint. (**Who, what, why**)

The Green Wine Co-Op has today launched a plastic wine bottle which it claims could help cut its carbon footprint. (**Who, when, what, why**)

Thanks to the help of a specialised US company, The Green Wine Co-Op has today launched a plastic wine bottle which it claims could help cut its carbon footprint. (**How, who, when, what, why**)

The Green Wine Co-Op announced today that it has teamed up with a US company to launch a plastic wine bottle in the UK which it claims could help cut its carbon footprint. (**Who, when, how, what, where, why**)

By deconstructing the news writing technique in this way it's much easier to pick out the different elements that make up the intro. And as you can see from the examples above, there is no set order

for the WWWWWH. It's up to you – as the writer
– to decide what order they should be put in.

Here's the background to that fishy story
spotted by *The Daily Grind*: **Fish disease
outbreaks confirmed**:

- Researchers from the government's Environment Agency are concerned about the health of fish in rivers across England.
- It seems anglers have reported seeing fish floating on the surface.
- On inspection, researchers found that the fish had contracted a highly contagious disease.
- There are fears the disease could spread across the country.
- If left unchecked, it could wipe out fish stocks.
- Angling has been suspended in these infected areas.
- There is no threat to human health.

Once again, let's use WWWWWH to figure out the
story:

Who: Who is this story about? The 'who' in
this case is *the Environment Agency*.

What: What is the story about? What's important?
There's an outbreak of a nasty fish disease that could spread across the country.

Why: Why is this story important? Why is it happening?
If left unchecked, it could wipe out fish stocks.

Where: Where is it taking place?
In rivers across England

When: When is it taking place?
Now

How: How is it happening? A better how question might be: How are they hoping to combat this problem?
There are restrictions in place to halt the spread of the disease.

Now that we've identified the key elements, it's time to pull the different pieces of information together to make the story. Once again, there is no set order to the WWWWWH. It's more a question of where they fit in best. As with many aspects of writing, this is down to the writer. However, a good rule of thumb is to begin by putting the WWWWWH elements in order of their importance:

An outbreak of a fish disease (**What**)

An outbreak of a fish disease has been found in rivers across England. (**What, where**)

An outbreak of a fish disease, which if left unchecked could wipe out fish stocks, has been found in rivers across England. (**What, why, where**)

An outbreak of a fish disease, which if left unchecked could wipe out fish stocks, has been found in rivers across England, the Environment Agency has confirmed. (**What, why, where, who**)

An outbreak of a fish disease, which if left unchecked could wipe out fish stocks, has been discovered in rivers across England, the Environment Agency confirmed today. (**What, why, where, who, when**)

Anglers have been banned from fishing in rivers across England following the outbreak of a fish disease, which, if left unchecked could wipe out fish stocks, the Environment Agency confirmed today. (**How, where, what, why, who, when**)

Once again, this story has been built up piece-by-piece, element-by-element until the whole story has effectively been wrapped up in one single sentence.

Yes, it's awkward to start with – and a little cumbersome – but the outcome is concise and neatly boxed.

The one thing that links all the examples so far is that they are all factual and to the point. There is no wordplay. Of course, some of the words could be spiced up to make the language more colourful, but that is for later. The important first stage is to be able to grapple with all the different WWWWWH elements and put them together into a meaningful sentence. Here's another example to think about, with the headline ***Priceless grand piano broken:***

- Earlier this week, a priceless grand piano was being transported by lorry to a music festival in Shropshire.
- As workmen nudged the piano onto the lift at the rear of the lorry, they lost balance and the piano lurched to the left before sliding off and hitting the ground.
- Despite its heavy cast-iron frame, the piano lay smashed to bits on the ground.
- The noise of the twisted frame and mangled wires rang out loud like some tormented animal.

As before, we can break down the WWWWWH elements into the following:

Who: *A priceless piano*

What: *Smashed beyond repair*

Why: *It was an accident*

Where: *Shropshire*

When: *Earlier this week*

How: *Dropped off the back of a lorry*

Put them all together and we end up with:

A priceless grand piano has been smashed beyond repair after it was accidentally dropped off the back of a lorry in Shropshire earlier this week.

Once again, all the WWWWWH elements are there, distilling the story into a single, crystal clear sentence. But you may have noticed that some of the information provided – namely, the sound of the 'twisted frame and mangled wires' that 'rang out loud like some tormented animal' – has been omitted. On the face of it, this would make a dramatic addition to the story. But since it does not easily match any of the WWWWWH elements that we've identified, it doesn't quite seem to fit the structure we're working to – however appealing it might be. Which provides a couple of interesting rules – for now at least:

- You can't include every single detail in a sentence, however hard you try.
- Following that logic, some things – however attractive – have to be left out (to start with at least, though they may be included later).
- It's down to the writer – that's you – to make that judgement call.

Later on, we'll see how these rules can be bent or even broken. But that's for later. Here's one last example to show how the structure works, under the headline *A **super storm brewing in mid Atlantic***:

> **Who:** *A super storm*
>
> **What:** *Heading for the UK*
>
> **Why:** *It could cause serious damage*
>
> **Where:** *The UK*
>
> **When:** *Imminently*
>
> **How:** *Brewing in the mid Atlantic*

Put it all together and you get:

> *A super storm brewing in the mid Atlantic could cause serious damage to the UK when it makes landfall later today.*

One sentence – 21 words, that's all – has summed up a weather event that could wreak havoc on the UK, causing damage to property and threatening people's lives. Arguably, the matter-of-fact language doesn't convey the severity of what could happen when the approaching super storm hits the coast. But at this stage in learning the news writing technique, it's not meant to. The important thing at this point is to identify the key elements and write them in a grammatically correct sentence.

All these examples of a WWWWWH summary sentence share one thing in common – they distil the story into one sentence. One nugget. One thought. Being able to do this with any piece of writing is a major milestone for anyone who wants to improve his or her professional communication skills. It means you've taken time and trouble to digest and understand what you're writing about, and then break it down into what's really important. Or, in other words, it shows that you are thinking about your reader. Think about it. If you, as the author of a letter or email, for example, find identifying and pulling together the relevant information difficult, imagine how your readers might feel if they have to work it out for themselves?

For me, the most important part of this is that by working methodically this way, anyone can interrogate a story and come up with the most important and relevant pieces of information. It's a stage in the writing process that should not be overlooked because failure to assemble all the relevant information will always lead to difficulty later on.

It's not just about structure

All these examples illustrate how to approach any story, identify the key parts and then put them together in one neat sentence. It's effective, but if you're new to it, it can be unwieldy at times. And in some cases, figuring out the WWWWWH can lead to a lot of head scratching. But, like most things in life, it simply takes practice. The more you do it, the easier it becomes.

At first, it might seem as if you're taking a backward step. Don't worry. Stick with it, because soon something strange will start to happen. Now that you've been shown the technique, you'll begin to spot it when you read news articles.

By looking beyond the words and seeing the structure, you'll soon be able to see inside a story. You'll be blessed with a kind of editorial X-ray vision. And as you begin to hone this skill, you'll be able to spot the technique, not just in news stories but also in letters, blogs, reports, emails – anything that's written well.

Equally, you'll be able to see when this method is not used and the impact this can have on a piece of writing. When this happens, you'll know that this methodology has started to become an embedded part of your writing.

I cannot stress enough how important it is to adopt and understand this process. The news writing technique is the structural engineering that underpins all good writing. It may seem clunky to start with, but maintaining structural integrity is vital – just as it is for a building. After all, we don't want our building – or our stories – to come crashing down around our ears. But this is only the beginning.

Once you've got to grips with being able to sum up a story in a sentence or two, the next thing to grasp is how to extend this and provide more information. In the next chapter we will look at how to build on this framework and turn it into something that is more interesting and has greater colour.

Think about it

1 Find three different examples of pieces of writing you have seen this week, perhaps a short newspaper article, an email and a report. Look at the structure of each of them and see if you can identify the WWWWWH elements of the opening sentences and the order in which they have been placed. How effective are these pieces of writing in putting across their message?

2 Can you identify the WWWWWH elements in this story?

An amateur astronomer in the US claims to have discovered a new planet in a galaxy far, far away from Earth. It was discovered using a $100 telescope in his back garden. After checking the data and cross-referencing it with other stargazers, scientists in Colorado have confirmed that the new planet – which *has two moons – does exist. The new discovery has been recorded as 'ES7359'. Speaking earlier this week at a news conference, they say the discovery is important because it shows that with even basic resources it is still possible for ordinary people to make important scientific discoveries.*

3 Look back at the intro to the *Priceless grand piano broken* story on page 32. What other information would you like to have as a reader?

Suggested answer to question 2:
Who: *An amateur astronomer*
What: *Discovered a new planet with two moons*
Why: *It shows that anyone can make scientific discoveries*
Where: *The US*
When: *Recently*
How: *By using a cheap telescope in his back garden*

---

3 Enticing people to read on

So far we have looked at the structure of a news story and the importance of the inverted triangle. This is key because it gives you a framework and allows you to identify the raw materials to begin writing. But having the structure – or different elements – in place is only part of the story. Now it's time to improve the look and feel of our intro to make it more appealing to readers.

When it comes to news writing, the intro is the most important part of the story. Why? Because it presents information in a clear and methodical way. By summing up the story in a sentence or two, you can be sure that even if the reader doesn't read on, at least they leave with the most important information. But you want them to read on. The problem is, you only have a few seconds to convince them that your piece of writing is worth reading. To do that – and to help you refine your writing – there are three key things to remember:

- Use your best words.
- Think of an angle.
- Say it up front.

Let's look at these in a bit more detail.

Use your best words

It goes without saying that word selection is very important. The words you use can lift your text off the page and elevate it to somewhere special. Or, they can leave the reader feeling uninspired. One of the best ways to ensure that you use your best words and phrases is to play a simple game of word association.

Whatever you write about, there will be some word associations that could add a little sparkle to your text. For some people, this comes naturally, and words just pop into their heads. For others, it's more of a struggle. No matter. If word association is something that doesn't come naturally to you, then consider jotting down a few useful words before you start writing in order to build up some potential vocabulary.

For instance, in the last chapter we heard about The Green Wine Co-Op's decision to use plastic bottles for its wine. That prompts me to think of words such as *wine, wine bottle, cork, corkscrew, carafe, mulled wine, vintage, Bordeaux, Chardonnay, grapes, sour grapes, off-licence, green, nose, bouquet, connoisseurs, vino, rosé, bottle banks, glass, smashing* ... The company's decision to reduce its carbon footprint makes me think of words and phrases like *green, environmental, eco warrior, eco-friendly, climate change, biomass, sustainable, biodegradable* ...

By spending a little time creating a personalised set of vocabulary, I can now start to revise my intro. So, instead of:

> *The Green Wine Co-Op has launched a plastic wine bottle which it claims could help cut its carbon footprint.*

we could have:

> *The Green Wine Co-Op has **uncorked** a plastic wine bottle which it claims could help cut its carbon footprint.*

> *The Green Wine Co-Op has **popped the cork** on a plastic wine bottle as part of its plan to cut carbon emissions.*

> *The Green Wine Co-Op has **popped the cork** on an **eco-friendly** plastic wine bottle as part of **ambitious** plans to **slash** its carbon emissions.*

Simply by using more interesting language, the launch of a plastic wine bottle becomes a cork-popping party in celebration of an eco-friendly initiative.

The extent to which you decide to use language to lift your text depends on a number of things that are discussed in Chapter 7. In essence, though, how far you push this element of creativity depends on your audience, the reason for writing and what format that writing takes. Over time, you'll develop a feel for what's right and what's wrong. A set of words that are perfectly acceptable in an ad campaign aimed at young people may not be right to describe the same product to shareholders.

My personal preference is 'less is more'. If there's too much wordplay, the language can get in the way of what you're trying to say.

Let's look at the story that focuses on the outbreak of a deadly fish virus. Here are four possible intros, each slightly different:

> *Anglers have been banned from fishing in rivers across England following the outbreak of a fish disease, which, if left unchecked, could wipe out fish stocks, the Environment Agency confirmed today.*

> *Anglers have been banned from fishing in rivers across England following the outbreak of a **deadly** fish disease, which, if left unchecked, could wipe out fish stocks, the Environment Agency confirmed today.*

> *Anglers have been banned from fishing in rivers across England following the outbreak of a **killer** fish disease, which, if left unchecked, could wipe out fish stocks, the Environment Agency confirmed today.*

*Anglers have been banned from fishing in
rivers across England following the
outbreak of a **killer** fish disease, which, if
left unchecked, could wipe out fish stocks,
the Environment Agency **warned** today.*

As you can see, just changing one or two words can
make a huge difference. This isn't just any disease,
it's a *deadly* or *killer* disease. The Environment
Agency didn't just make an announcement, it
warned people.

The use of more colourful and interesting language
while maintaining the original structure makes the
story more compelling. It doesn't need to be a
wholesale rewrite – sometimes just a word here or
there is enough.

And what about that piano? What words can we change to give the story more impact? Here is the original intro, followed by three subtle re-writes:

> *A priceless grand piano has been smashed beyond repair after it was accidentally dropped off the back of a lorry in Shropshire earlier this week.*
>
> *A priceless grand piano has been smashed into a **thousand pieces** after it was accidentally dropped off the back of a lorry in Shropshire earlier this week.*
>
> *A priceless grand piano has been smashed into a **thousand pieces** after it accidentally **slipped** off the back of a lorry in Shropshire earlier this week.*
>
> *A priceless grand piano **hit a bum note** earlier this week when it **slid** off the back of a lorry in Shropshire and smashed into a **thousand pieces**.*

As you can see, the selection of different words adds colour to the story without actually altering the structure very much. The addition of a musical pun (*bum note*) merely adds to the stomach-wrenching tragedy of what happened. And if you go one step further and include in the next sentence the sound made by the piano as it hit the ground, you end up with something even more compelling:

> *A priceless grand piano has been smashed into a **thousand pieces** after it accidentally **slipped** off the back of a lorry in Shropshire earlier this week. Onlookers said that the frame twisted and buckled as it hit the ground, making a sound like 'some tormented animal'.*

Using your best words not only lifts the text, it also increases the chances of your reader deciding to read your story in its entirety. So, your intro now has two functions:

- To sum up the story in one digestible sentence.
- To be so compelling that the reader wants to read on.

So, what's your angle?

Clearly, being creative with words can help bring some shine to a text, but it's not the only way to achieve this. I've trained people who cross their arms and tell me in no uncertain terms that the use of creative language is not for them. Their approach to writing, they tell me, is more factual. They are uncomfortable using a palate of more colourful language. But this is not a problem.

Being creative isn't just about using flowery language. You can be equally creative by getting the right angle. In other words, you can also make a reader sit up and take notice by approaching a story from a different perspective. For instance, instead of:

> The Green Wine Co-Op has popped the cork on an **eco-friendly** plastic wine bottle as part of **ambitious** plans to **slash** its carbon emissions.

you could change the angle of the story so that it is written from the wine drinkers' perspective:

> Wine drinkers can now do their bit for the environment after The Green Wine Co-Op launched a new plastic wine bottle.

or:

> Wine drinkers are being assured that the taste of their favourite vintage will not be affected following The Green Wine Co-Op's decision to use recyclable plastic bottles instead of glass.

Add in a little creative language and you could get this:

> **Chardonnay-sipping** wine drinkers can now do their bit for the environment after The Green Wine Co-Op launched a new **eco-friendly** plastic wine bottle.

or:

*Wine **connoisseurs** are being assured that the taste of their favourite **Merlot** will not be affected following The Green Wine Co-Op's decision to use recyclable plastic bottles instead of glass.*

Playing with angles is all about creative thinking – not creative words. What about toying with a different environmental angle that has yet to be highlighted?

The ancient cork-producing oak forests of Sardinia could be under threat after The Green Wine Co-Op became the latest retailer to ditch traditional glass wine bottles in favour of recyclable plastic containers.

Cork from Sardinian oak trees is famed for its use in wine bottles. But with the advent of plastic bottles, there are fears cork farmers could be put out of business and the forests lost forever.

Some people might describe this as coming from left field or 'thinking outside of the box'. To me, it's simply what is possible once you appreciate the role that different angles can play. It's not a 'gift' or down to the fact that someone is 'good with words'. It's about a thought process that, once you understand some of the rules, you can explore and exploit.

Even the fishy tale about a killer disease can benefit from a different angle:

> *Government scientists have sought to reassure people across England that the outbreak of a deadly fish virus poses no threat to human health.*

And what about our world-famous grand piano?

> *Festival organisers were – quite literally – left picking up the pieces after their priceless grand piano fell off the back of a lorry, shattering into a pile of keys, mangled metal and wood. The incident happened as removal men were completing the last leg of an epic journey transporting the instrument from Germany to Shropshire.*

The beauty of the 'angle' is that it's all about the way you think. It doesn't matter if you're not creative with words. Even if you class yourself as a more methodical and structured writer, you can still produce interesting copy.

Creativity comes in many shapes and forms. It may be that your creativity comes from your use of language, word play and puns. Or it may be that your individualism comes from your ability to see stories from different angles. On their own, each is a powerful tool when it comes to producing copy. Together, they can take your writing to a new height of skill.

Say it up front

Every single word you write has the ability to capture the imagination of your readers and reel them in. Equally, by being evasive or not ordering your words correctly, the greater chance you have of alienating your readers. Take this intro, for example:

> *According to research published today by HappyCo – the UK's leading lifestyle and wellbeing institution with offices in Lanarkshire, Scotland and in the south of France, which last year launched its happiness index to monitor the nation's well-being – Monday is the most miserable day of the week.*

Talk about long-winded! Yes, this intro contains WWWWWH, so technically it's correct. The snag is, it takes 39 words before the reader gets to the main point, which is:

> *According to research published by HappyCo, Monday is the most miserable day of the week.*

Or even better:

Monday is the most miserable day of the week, according to research published by HappyCo.

Earlier, I touched on how the news writing technique is a way of being kind to your readers, making it as easy as possible for them to access the information they're after. This is a perfect example of the kind of refinement you need to be an effective writer.

If you understand news writing, you'll spot the problem in an instant. And with just a quick change here and there, you'll be able to create editorial gold. But it's not alchemy that makes it happen – it's simply about understanding this technique.

That's the beauty of news writing. It has structure, form and rules. It instils a level of discipline in anyone who is prepared to add this technique to their quiver of writing skills. Despite its seemingly rigid structure, it is, in fact, extremely flexible and provides scope for outstanding creativity.

Think about it

Here is an extract from a survey commissioned by HappyCo:

How happy are you?

With all the doom and gloom around at the moment, more and more people are asking themselves the same question: How happy am I? A survey by HappyCo found:

67% of people admit to lying in bed at night worrying about their lives.

71% of people believe happiness is more important than money.

23% of people said they would take a 'substantial' pay cut if it meant they could be happier.

85% of people said having more holidays would make them happier.

---

1 Brainstorm some words that you might be able to use in a story about this survey.

2 Can you spot any different angles from which the story could be written?

3 Have a go at writing a few intros based on what you've come up with. Experiment with them. In your opinion, which are better and why?

4 Breaking the rules

The news writing technique dictates that we say everything up front in the first sentence or two, using the all-important WWWWWH structure. However, if you've tried this technique for yourself – and tried to get all of the WWWWWH elements into your opening sentence – you'll no doubt have come to the conclusion that it can be, at times, difficult to do. Indeed, for some stories it can be bordering on the impossible. As good as it is, it can sometimes be a bit, well, clunky.

So, here's the magic of the news writing technique. Once you've learnt how to do it … once you've mastered the method … once you've accepted the discipline of news writing … once you can get WWWWWH into a single sentence … you can start breaking the rules. Of course, that does not give you the green light to run amok and do whatever you like. But it does mean that you have more freedom than you might think. Yes, you can bend the rules. Yes, you can break them! But you must do it correctly. The skill is to understand what rule you are breaking and why. By doing so, you will begin to master news writing.

Omitting some WWWWWH

Let's go back to the plastic wine bottle story. Technically, it's an example of a news intro because it contains WWWWWH:

> *The Green Wine Co-Op announced today that it has teamed up with a US company to launch a plastic wine bottle in the UK, a move which it claims could help cut its carbon footprint.*

But, we can eliminate some elements of WWWWWH without damaging the integrity of the intro. Firstly, we can remove the When …

> *The Green Wine Co-Op ~~announced today that it~~ has teamed up with a US company to launch a plastic wine bottle in the UK which it claims could help cut its carbon footprint.*

So now it reads:

> *The Green Wine Co-Op has teamed up with a US company to launch a plastic wine bottle in the UK which it claims could help cut its carbon footprint.*

We don't need an explicit When because it's there in the present perfect form has teamed up, which shows that the 'teaming up' has happened and is still ongoing.

And if The Green Wine Co-Op was a well-known brand that was a household name in the UK, we could also drop the *Where*:

> *The Green Wine Co-Op has teamed up with a US company to launch a plastic wine bottle* ~~in the UK~~ *which it claims could help cut its carbon footprint.*

So that it now reads:

> *The Green Wine Co-Op has teamed up with a US company to launch a plastic wine bottle which it claims could help cut its carbon footprint.*

Compared to the technically correct version we started with, this slimmed down version is much snappier without any loss of meaning. And yet it still holds its integrity. Here's another example that's worth looking at:

> *Firefighters in Dorset, England, reunited a dog with its owner yesterday after the pet went missing during a walk almost a fortnight ago.*
>
> *It's understood that Frank, a border terrier, raced away from his owner Jeremy Sanders after catching the scent of a rabbit. It's believed the dog got trapped after chasing the rabbit into its warren.*

Despite searching for hours, Mr Sanders failed to find Frank and put up posters in the area asking for people to contact him if they found the much-loved pet.

Mr Sanders heard nothing until earlier this week, when emergency services were called to an isolated stretch of farmland after passers-by heard strange noises coming from underground.

It was here that officers belonging to Dorset Fire Service found Frank stuck underground in a rabbit warren. Firefighters finally rescued Frank after an hour and – despite losing a third of his bodyweight – the border terrier was described as being fit and well.

To be fair, there's very little wrong with this story or the intro. It's all perfectly in place and neatly structured. But there are a few things that can be done to improve things. If this story is published in the UK, then surely people don't need to know that Dorset is in England – they should know that. We can also do away with *yesterday* as well, because we know it happened in the past, but we don't need to know exactly when. We can then change the past simple verb *reunited* to the present perfect form *have reunited*, which gives a more celebratory feel, because we know the dog and its owner are now together.

So, a few minor tweaks and the intro now reads:

Firefighters in Dorset have reunited a dog with its owner after the pet went missing during a walk almost a fortnight ago.

It's not an earth-shattering amendment, but it does ensure that the copy flows nicely. Of course, if this is aimed at an international audience, the inclusion of *England* or *in the UK* is essential so that people know where it happened. On the flipside, if the story was published in a local paper in Dorset, there would be no need to mention the county at all. Instead, it would read:

Local firefighters have reunited a dog with its owner after the pet went missing during a walk two weeks ago.

To many people, these might seem like minor, even insignificant changes. To me, it shows that the writer is thinking about his or her audience and varying the copy to match the readership.

In both these examples, it was the *where* and the *when* that were omitted. There are no hard and fast rules about which of the WWWWWH elements can be left out but, as a rule of thumb, these two elements tend to be the ones that put their hands up and shout 'Pick me, pick me!'

Which is all well and good, but what happens if you pick the wrong ones?

The perils of omitting the wrong element

We've just seen how, in the right circumstances, we can omit one or two of the WWWWWH elements without losing any of the meaning. Arguably, doing so actually creates something that is leaner and better for it.

But what happens if you remove the wrong element? Or to put it another way, deciding which of the WWWWWH to omit is not a lottery. It has to be thought out and decided. Because if you get it wrong, it can land you in hot water. As this next story reveals.

Bank hands out free cash

The boss of Shiretown Bank has said he plans to hand out crisp £10 notes to passers-by to say 'thank you' for people's ongoing support during the financial crisis.

In an announcement to the Stock Exchange, he said that despite difficult times, the bank's continued progress was testament to the support of its customers.

But critics said the decision to hand out free money was just a cheap publicity stunt and urged the bank to lend more money to hard-up businesses.

What a cracking story! A bank handing out free cash – there's a novelty! But there's a snag. What if you want to get your hands on this free cash? The story misses out the two most important elements of the WWWWWH. Exactly *where* the chief exec is going to be when he hands out the lolly and *when* he is doing it. Without this key information, the story is simply half-baked. And yet, it doesn't take much to put this right:

The boss of Shiretown Bank has said he plans to hand out crisp £10 notes to passers-by to say 'thank you' for people's ongoing support during the financial crisis.

CEO John Penny will be handing out the cash on the steps of the Bank of England tomorrow at 11.00 am.

In an announcement to the Stock Exchange, he said that despite difficult times, the bank's continued progress was testament to the support of its customers.

But critics said the decision to hand out free money was just a cheap publicity stunt and urged the bank to lend more money to hard-up businesses.

This simple addition fills the void in the previous story. But what if you want to give the *where* and the *when* more prominence? As the author, you might consider switching sentences:

The boss of Shiretown Bank – John Penny – will be handing out free £10 notes on the steps of the Bank of England tomorrow at 11.00 am.

He denied that the move was part of a PR stunt and insisted that the decision to hand out crisp £10 notes was a way to say 'thank you' for people's ongoing support during the financial crisis.

Here, far from being relegated, the *where* and the *when* get top billing in the intro. This approach leaves the reader in no doubt at all about what this author believes to be the most important part of the story. So which one is better? Which one of these two approaches is correct? The answer, as always, lies with the author. It's up to you. Clearly, the example that omitted the *when* and *where* is lacking two vital pieces of information. That said, if the story had been written in Australia about free dosh being handed out in the UK, then leaving out the *when* and *where* is neither here nor there – unless someone really wants to fly half way around the world just to pick up a tenner!

As for the corrected versions, deciding the order of the information is a matter of debate. The first version attempts to explain why the bank is going to hand out free money. The second is rather more grasping and tells you where to find it.

Breaking the rules when you have too much information

There are times when to fulfil a technically correct news introduction means that there is simply too much information for the reader to take in all at once. This can make the text very difficult to read and may obscure the main point.

Take this tragic story:

Final curtain for British movie star

Veronica Burton-Smythe – three-times Oscar-winning star of films such as 'All Along the Witchtower', 'From Here To Nonentity' and 'Dr Muchlove', who married and divorced on-screen leading man Jack Wellard no fewer than nine times before finally settling down with screenwriter Buster Type – has died at her home in Surrey after a short illness, surrounded by friends and family, her agent confirmed today.

Once again, this opening sentence is written in the news writing style and contains all the technically correct elements. But it's more than 60 words long; do we really need all of this information up front?

While there can be no doubt that the glittering career and colourful life of Veronica has kept audiences on the edge of their seats for decades, in this instance sometimes less is more.

Or in other words, when you strip down this message to its bare bones, all that is really needed is *who* and *what*:

> *Movie legend Veronica Burton-Smythe has died.*

But the result is a sentence that is too harsh and too abrupt. However, it can be softened, simply by adding the *where*:

> *Movie legend Veronica Burton-Smythe has died at her home in Surrey.*

Or even better:

> *Movie legend Veronica Burton-Smythe has died peacefully at her home in Surrey, surrounded by friends and family.*

At this stage, the inclusion of all the details of her colourful life merely gets in the way of what is a sad story. That is not to say it is unimportant. Far from it. It is this colourful information that will leave readers with a smile on their face as they remember with fondness this star of the silver screen:

Movie legend Veronica Burton-Smythe has died peacefully at her home in Surrey, surrounded by friends and family.

The three-times Oscar-winning star of films such as 'All Along the Witchtower', 'From Here To Nonentity' and 'Dr Muchlove' was a national treasure, and her career spanned more than 60 years on the silver screen.

The movie starlet's private life was almost as colourful as her on-screen appearances, famously marrying and divorcing leading man Jack Wellard no fewer than nine times. In 1997, she finally settled down with screenwriter Buster Type and devoted much of her time to growing roses.

'This much-loved actress will be greatly missed,' her agent said today.

When you first learn the basics of the news writing technique, the technically correct thing to do is to include all the elements of WWWWWH. But as we've discovered, this can be difficult to do. So, omitting some of the elements is OK, so long as the integrity of the story remains, as in the case of Frank the border terrier.

Or you could look at it another way. Instead of deleting elements, you could start with a blank sheet of paper and make a decision about which of the WWWWWH elements need to be included, as in the case of movie legend Veronica Burton-Smythe. Both techniques are fine, and it's up to you which one you use, as long as the result maintains the integrity of a well-written intro.

Spreading WWWWWH over two sentences

There are times when you might want to spread the WWWWWH elements over two – or maybe three – sentences. That's fine, provided you understand that the longer it takes to get to the point, the greater the chance you have of losing your reader. That said, the advantage of this more relaxed approach is that it does give the writer scope to provide some supplementary information that may otherwise be put in subsequent paragraphs.

The following story talks about the growth in 3D printing:

3D printing shows real depth

It is estimated that the 3D printing industry is now worth more than $3.7 billion a year, according to research published today.

Experts believe this figure is likely to grow by 15% a year as 3D printing is adopted by car manufacturers and aerospace industries.

*The take-up of 3D printing technology is
growing at such a pace some experts predict
that it could revolutionise the way
companies manufacture products. Indeed,
some claim that manufacturing could
happen in the home, with people printing
their own products from a catalogue of
items.*

*3D printing is the process of making a three-
dimensional solid object such as a cup and
saucer from a digital model.*

As you will have gathered, the story is written in
the news style with the most important information
– the 3D printing industry is now worth more than
$3.7 billion – firmly at the top. Technically, it's
well written and to the point. But there's a problem.
What if readers don't know what 3D printing is? If
that's the case, then the model that we have used
needs to be altered to help compensate. In effect,
we need to explain what 3D printing is from the
outset. We need to break one of the rules:

*The industry behind 3D printing – the
process of making three-dimensional solid
objects such as a cup and saucer from a
digital model – is now estimated to be worth
more than $3.7 billion, according to
research published today.*

Experts believe this figure is likely to grow by 15% a year as 3D printing is adopted by car manufacturers and aerospace industries.

The adoption of 3D printing technology is growing at such a pace that some experts predict it could revolutionise the way companies manufacture products. Indeed, some claim that manufacturing could happen in the home, with people printing their own products from a catalogue of items.

Arguably, this is an improvement on the first version since it now explains what 3D printing is up front. But the result is that the sentence is 40 words long. Depending on the publication, that may or may not be acceptable. To make it more digestible, we could break down the opening sentence so that the reader gets 'the story' in the first two sentences rather than one:

The industry behind 3D printing – the process of making three-dimensional solid objects such as a cup and saucer from a digital model – is growing at a record rate.

It is estimated that the industry is worth more than $3.7 billion, according to research published today.

As you can see, splitting the WWWWWH, and even relegating some of the elements, is allowed. Indeed, in some cases it is to be encouraged. The skill of an informed writer is to understand what you're doing and why you're doing it. To do so, you're making a judgement call – you're not acting on a whim or because you've plucked something out of thin air or because something just 'came to you' – your decision is based on something of substance.

It's impossible to say which elements have to be retained and which can be reserved for following paragraphs. The way you break the rules for one story can differ enormously compared with another.

Even the plastic wine bottle story can be split over two sentences:

> *The UK-based Green Wine Co-Op – which last year opened more than a dozen shops in France – announced today that it has teamed up with a US company. The transatlantic tie-up heralds the launch of a plastic wine bottle which both companies say will help cut carbon emissions.*

By shifting the emphasis and moving ideas around, it's possible to play with the structure of news writing. You should feel free to experiment with this yourself and be resourceful with the technique.

The more you understand what works – and what doesn't – the better you will become.

The first three chapters of this book concentrated on the technically correct news writing style, using the WWWWWH inverted triangle approach. To improve your skill as a writer, this approach is something that should be practised and honed continuously. The more you do it, the better you will become. And once you have the technique under your belt, you can start to learn how to break the rules. What you need to remember, though, is that omitting any of the WWWWWH comes at a price. It is only by understanding the rules that you can break them.

From all these examples, we can draw a few conclusions about the use of WWWWWH:

- Although it's technically correct to use all six of the WWWWWH elements in an intro, in reality, you don't have to. Depending on the story, some elements of the WWWWWH are more important than others. You can pick and choose from them, based on their relevance to the story. That said, just because some of them are less important than others, it doesn't mean they are redundant. It just means they can be inserted into the story later on.

- There is no set order for WWWWWH. They can be in whatever order you like but, ideally, you do need at least two of the six for your intro to make any sense.
- You can split the WWWWWH elements over two sentences if that helps.
- If you break the rules, you have to know what you're doing and why you're doing it.

Have a go!

1 Pick up a newspaper or magazine and find a couple of stories you like. Try to re-write the intros by adapting what's there. Mix and match the WWWWWH – and spread them over two or three sentences if necessary – to create something new. How does your new version of the story compare to the original?

2 Do the same exercise with some of your own material – be it an essay, email or letter. How does it compare to your original?

5 Beyond the intro: building your story

So far, we've looked at the news writing intro and the different ways this can be manipulated to make an interesting and worthwhile beginning to a story. Arguably, the intro is the most important part of any news style story because success or failure here determines whether the reader reads on or not. Whether you adhere religiously to the WWWWWH structure or prefer to play with it is up to you. But if you have crafted your intro correctly, the rest of the story should almost write itself. That is, as long as you stick to the other rule of the news story – namely, that like the shape of the inverted triangle, information is introduced in descending order of importance. And who makes the decision about what's important and what's not? You do. The author. The writer. It's your job to make that judgement call.

By adding supporting information bit by bit, you help to build the story. The information you add could give more detail; it could support the story or it might introduce an element of discussion and thereby help to add balance. What you add is down to you. Quotes – if appropriate – are also great because they can add colour to a story.

To see how the news story can be fleshed out, here's the free cash story in full:

Bank hands out free cash

The boss of Shiretown Bank is to hand out crisp £10 notes to passers-by to say 'thank you' for people's ongoing support during the financial crisis.

CEO John Penny will be handing out the cash on the steps of the Bank of England tomorrow at 11.00 am, it was confirmed today.

In an announcement to the Stock Exchange, Penny said that despite difficult times, the bank's continued progress was testament to the support of its customers.

'No one can doubt the difficulties we've faced,' said Mr Penny, 'but I'm confident we've weathered the worst of the financial storm.'

But critics were quick to jump on the announcement, saying that the bank's decision to hand out free money was just a cheap publicity stunt.

Erica Jones of the pressure group 'Go Bankers' urged the bank to lend more money to hard-up businesses instead of handing out £10 notes to passers-by.

Asked whether she would accept one of the free tenners, Ms Jones said: 'Yes, but I intend to give it away to someone who really needs it.'

So there you have it – a story that talks about the bank handing out free £10 notes. It's a much fuller story with more information, notably the fact that while some might consider free money a 'good news' story, there are some who would disagree.

So, does this mean that if two people were given the same information, they would, in effect, produce the same story? No! Absolutely not! Why? Because it depends on the angle they take and the importance they attach to certain facts.

Here's that bank story again:

The CEO of Shiretown Bank has been ridiculed after promising to hand out free £10 notes to members of the public.

Erica Jones – from the pressure group 'Go Bankers' – said the move was nothing more than a cheap publicity stunt designed to generate positive headlines.

Instead, she urged the bank to be more responsible and to lend more money to hard-up businesses.

In this example, there is no balance: no mention of where or when the money will be handed out, no space devoted to why the bank is embarking on this action. Instead, it is solely an anti-bank polemic. And yet, it could be so much more.

Whatever the rights and wrongs of that approach, what this shows is that the same story can be written in many different ways, depending on the angle and the hierarchy of information that is used. All these things are down to the author.

Here's another example:

Last year a young man, Jack Butler, stole a car and went joyriding. Approaching a known accident blackspot, he lost control of the vehicle and plunged 30ft down a bank into a tree.

Emergency services were called to the accident and it took three hours to cut him out before he was flown by air ambulance to a local hospital where he received specialist treatment for multiple fractures and a collapsed lung. Butler was lucky to survive.

The car was a write-off. The whole operation – including a three-month stay in hospital – is estimated to have cost £250,000. The 18 year old was sentenced to six months in jail. When he was released, he vowed to walk from John O'Groats to Land's End to raise money so he could pay back his debt to society.

There are a number of different angles and approaches you can take with this story. And each version of the story will unfurl in a different way, depending on the angle or approach taken. For instance, you could have:

An 18-year-old convicted car thief is planning to raise £250,000 for charity after he was involved in a near-fatal crash at a well-known accident blackspot.

Jack Butler plans to walk from John O'Groats to Land's End as a way of paying back the emergency services for rescuing him. He also wants to thank the doctors and nurses at Finchdean Hospital for saving his life.

Speaking as he left prison today, the 18 year old – who admits he's lucky to be alive – said: 'I've spent the last six months in jail thinking about how I can pay back my debt to society. I can't think of a better way than to raise money for the air ambulance, the fire service and the local hospital.'

This approach is sympathetic to the young tearaway, giving him the opportunity to make amends, with the subsequent paragraphs appearing to support that premise. But that is just one angle. How about this one?

A hospital specialist has raised concerns about the welfare of a young man who has decided to walk from John O'Groats to Land's End to raise money for charity.

Dr Marie Edwards, who works at Finchdean
Hospital, said the marathon hike could
cause irreparable damage to the young man.
She maintained that he was still not fully
recovered from his injuries.

'Jack Butler is not a well man, and this walk
– plus carrying a heavy backpack – could
lead to permanent damage to his spine,' said
Dr Edwards.

So, here we have a completely different approach
that doesn't even mention the fact that Jack Butler
was involved in a car smash – or even that he spent
six months doing time for his crime. No matter.
What's important to understand is that regardless of
the approach taken, each story has a natural flow,
depending on your starting point.

These first five chapters have summed up
the news writitng style. We are now going on to
use this as a foundation for looking at alternative
ways of structuring your writing and introducing
more freedom without forgetting the basic
principles. Let's conclude with what we have learnt
so far:

- News writing involves structuring a
  story by using WWWWWH.
- The news writing structure can be
  represented by an inverted triangle,
  showing that information is ordered in

a hierarchy, with the most important coming first.

- The WWWWWH elements can be put in any order and are enhanced by the use of creative language and the angle you take.
- News writing is not a rigid structure: there is scope for great flexibility and creativity.
- Breaking the rules of the news writing technique is something to be encouraged, but only if you know what you're doing and keep the needs of your reader in mind.

Have a go!

Write a story in the news style using the information on the following page:

1 Start with the intro and then add more and more information to support the story. Make sure the information is in decreasing order of importance and that the story is no more than 100–150 words.

2 Then re-write it, this time from a different angle or perspective.

3 If you can, write a third story, once again of between 100–150 words and again from a different angle. Which do you prefer and why?

According to the latest research:

There are more than 1.75 billion smartphones in the world.

23% of adults admit that they don't know how to use them properly.

13% of adults said they had never downloaded an app.

Of those who had downloaded an app, 64% said they only played games on their smartphone.

53% of adults said they did not security-lock their phones, with 19% worried that they were likely to forget their PIN number.

78% of adults complained that the writing on the screens was too small.

43% of those quizzed said they would be happy with an old-fashioned mobile phone without apps, email, internet access, etc.

Tip: It's up to you to choose what you think is the most interesting part of the research – and therefore what comes first. It could be the fact that the number of smartphones now stands at more than 1.75 billion, or it could be that almost half of adults (43%) with a smartphone would prefer something less sophisticated. Then again, it could be the security issue that is of interest. You decide!

6 The 'drop intro'

So far, we've looked at the disciplined, structured approach of news writing, where you say what you want to say up front. But what if you want more freedom to express yourself or to set the scene? What if you need to introduce some ideas before getting to the punchline? One option is the 'drop intro' – and it's something you probably do already without realising it. As ever, the best way to describe a drop intro is to see one in action. Here's an example based on the now-familiar plastic wine bottle story:

> *There are few things in life more embarrassing than the clinking walk of shame. Whether it's carrier bags full of empties or a box with the bottles neatly stacked, the effect is the same. The weekly visit to the bottle bank is something that few of us relish as we attempt to get rid of the evidence of a wine-infused lifestyle. But all that could soon change.*
>
> **That's because The Green Wine Co-Op has recently announced plans to sell some of its wines in plastic bottles as part of an initiative to help cut carbon emissions.**

At no point during the first paragraph – made up of four sentences – do you 'get' the story. Unlike the news writing technique, it's not until you read the second paragraph that the real story unfolds. And why is it called a drop intro? Because the intro – that bit in bold – has been 'dropped' down the copy. It's a great technique for setting the scene, for entertaining your readers and engaging with them. For a writer, it offers greater scope for creativity and inventiveness, and it is often used by feature writers rather than news reporters.

In journalism, the drop intro is often referred to as being made up of two parts – the 'hook' and the 'nub'. The hook is the opening paragraph; it's designed to grab the reader's attention before getting to the nub or meat of the story. Here's another example, based on the free cash story:

> *To some, it was a much-welcomed gesture in these austere times. To others, it was a cynical PR stunt that merely reinforced their contempt for the UK's once-great financial institutions. Whatever your position, it certainly drew a crowd. Then again, Shiretown Bank CEO John Penny has always had a flair for the theatrical.*
>
> ***But his decision to hand out crisp ten-pound notes on the steps of the Bank of England was always going to be controversial.***

Once again, it takes four sentences and more than 50 words to get to the point of the story. The meat of the story – or the nub – has been dropped down the text. And here's one more example, based on a new story:

> *In this digital world of tablets and apps, you'd expect something more hi-tech from the experts at the UK Business School.* ***But according to their latest report, if you want to succeed in business you need to make a list – and stick to it.***

Again, it's a drop intro, but this time the hook is only made up of one sentence or 21 words. Which just goes to show that a drop intro doesn't have to be long. For the record, a news writing style intro based on the above would look something like this:

> *If you want to be successful in business, you need to make lists, prioritise tasks and then complete them. So say experts at the UK Business School ...*

In all three examples, the nub or crux of the story is dropped down the copy. The length of the drop intro could be several sentences or, as in the last example, it could be just a single sentence.

In my experience, most people who haven't had any formal writing training tend to write this way. It's a storytelling technique, rather than the structured, has-to-be-learnt news writing approach. It allows the writer to slide into the story, rather than diving in head-first. I remember in one writing workshop when I introduced the drop, a lady who worked in a busy marketing department, said: 'That's what I do! I write drops. I always write drops. I didn't know I wrote drops but now I know. I don't like the up-front news approach, I like the drop. That's what I do.'

Despite a protracted conversation, she was fixed on the idea that she wrote – and would only write – drop intros. To me, to shun one or other of these writing approaches is the same as saying: 'I love driving cars. Absolutely love it! But I only like turning left. I never turn right.'

The skill of the writer is to master both techniques, understand their function and use them accordingly.

How long should a drop intro be?

When drop intros are done well, they can grab a reader by the throat and get them begging for more. Or they can tease a reader and draw them in slowly and seductively. But there is a downside. What if your reader isn't drawn in? What if your reader gets bored, gives up and doesn't make it to the nub? Or what if your drop intro is simply too long? If that happens, your reader won't 'get' to the kernel of what you want to say, and your chance to be heard will have been missed. While the drop intro gives you far greater room for creativity, it is not without risk. For example:

> It must have been a difficult decision to make. After all, we are talking about someone's livelihood. But that has to be balanced against the welfare of others. Surely, no one can envy the decision they had to make. No doubt they had their suspicions. No doubt they carried out tests. And according to rigorous protocols put in place to minimise any errors, they double-checked them to make 100 per cent sure that they were confident of the result.

> Only then, were the men from the ministry prepared to put their reputation on the line to make a judgement call that could have devastating effects across the country.

> **But as the killer fish disease spreads, it's clear they had to take action and ban fishing ...**

The drop intro here is more than 100 words long. It may dabble with literary techniques like suspense and drama, but to me, it's a meandering self-indulgent piece of writing. To the untrained eye, this is simply 'waffle'. To those who understand the mechanics of writing structure, it's a drop intro that is far too long. Also, the hook hardly lives up to its name and fails to grab the reader's attention – which makes this an example of the worst case: a drop intro that is too long and also deadly dull.

That said, there is no hard and fast rule about the length of a drop intro. In general terms, the longer it is, the greater the chance you have of losing your reader. The shorter it is, the greater chance you have of getting your message across. Here's a short one-sentence hook:

The organisers of the Three Fields Music Festival spent five years raising enough money to ensure that a piano once played by Mozart could take centre stage at their annual event.

But the priceless piano will not be playing any part in this year's musical programme after delivery men dropped it off the back of a lorry, smashing it to pieces.

So there you have it: a drop intro ... about a dropped piano. As you can see, the shorter the hook, the quicker you get to the nub of the story – and the greater chance you have of keeping your reader. Does that mean you should avoid long drop intros? No. As long as you don't make your hook so long that your reader gets bored and gives up. Once again, it's a judgement call that only you, as the writer, can make.

Using angles to generate ideas

The *real* problem with drop intros is that they can be the cause of that dreaded ailment, writer's block. Let me explain. With the up-front news writing approach, you have a framework that helps you construct your story. By finding the WWWWWH and interlocking them together, you can write any story quickly. After all, that's why journalists are trained in this technique.

But write the same story using a drop intro and you – as the writer – have to come up with a preamble that allows you to lead up to the story. And this is why some people stare at a blank screen or piece of paper, not knowing where to start. But there is a remedy to the problem. And the answer lies in planning and assessing the different angles thrown up by each story. Let's look at the plastic wine bottle story again. In this example, which we saw earlier, the angle is the often embarrassing trip to the bottle bank to get rid of your empties.

There are few things in life more embarrassing than the clinking walk of shame. Whether it's carrier bags full of empties or a box with the bottles neatly stacked, the effect is the same. The weekly visit to the bottle bank is something that few of us relish as we attempt to get rid of the evidence of a wine-infused lifestyle. But all that could soon change.

That's because The Green Wine Co-Op has recently announced plans to sell some of its wines in plastic bottles as part of an initiative to help cut carbon emissions.

But, we could also focus on the environmental benefits of plastic wine bottles ... or the fact that plastic wine bottles don't alter the taste of the vino ... or how much easier this makes going on picnics because the bottles are so much lighter ... or how experts predict that sales of corkscrews are falling year-on-year because of the introduction of screw-top plastic wine bottles. By planning, by thinking of different angles, you can create different hooks leading to the same nub:

When people think about cutting CO2 emissions, many of them believe it involves switching off lights, turning down the thermostat and walking instead of driving to work. But one UK retailer has taken this a step further and shown that when it comes to being environmentally friendly, it's got lots of bottle.

That's because The Green Wine Co-Op has recently ...

Or:

For some wine buffs it may seem like a step too far. But if the proof of the pudding is in the eating, then the proof of this wine is in the drinking. And as you sip this rather elegant Chenin Blanc you'd never realise that not only are you drinking a particularly good vintage, you're also doing your bit for the environment.

That's because ...

Or:

With summer around the corner, now is the time to start thinking of picnics. Thankfully, lugging your hamper to some remote field or seaside spot should be easier, thanks to the introduction of lighter wine bottles.

That's because ...

Or:

It may have been said tongue-in-cheek, but the sentiment behind it is serious enough. It seems that as more and more wine is sold in plastic bottles, corkscrews are becoming increasingly redundant. Indeed, another line in the corkscrew's obituary has been written today.

That's because ...

As you can see, there is plenty of scope for creativity, depending on which angle you take. Knowing which of these is the right approach depends on you, why you're writing and your readership.

As for the rest of the story which follows the drop intro, that can still be based on the hierarchy of the news writing style. In fact, I would argue that this hierarchical approach is ideally suited to many writing tasks. That said, hierarchy is not the only structure that can be used. If you're writing a report or essay, for example, you may need a different approach.

Chronological order

It may be that the best way to present the information is in chronological order. In effect, something happens followed by something else to create a timeline or daisy chain of events. Done well, this approach is clear and logical.

Pros and cons

This is a popular approach for decision-makers, people in academia and those writing case studies and reports. By laying out the pros and cons, you can create a balanced appraisal before finishing with a conclusion or recommendation. When using this technique, don't be afraid to *signpost* the pros and cons so that the reader knows exactly what's what. For instance:

> *There are three reasons why this is important and they are first ... second ... and third ...*

Making the argument for/against

This is much like the structure for setting out the pros and cons of a subject. But whereas the pros and cons structure tends to be balanced, building an argument either in favour or against something tends to be more one-sided. As before, each supporting part of the argument should be signposted so that the reader knows exactly what's going on. It's a particularly useful approach for sales and marketing material that allows you to highlight the features of a product or service.

Over-arching

This is not dissimilar to the previous structure, except that it has an over-arching statement at the beginning, which is then supported by subsequent evidence. In effect, you're making the case for a particular stance or outlook. For instance:

> *Our new financial software is the best on the market and here's why.*

Step-by-step

Not dissimilar to the chronological approach, the step-by-step structure is all about a methodical approach, and it's particularly useful if you want to give someone instructions. Just make sure you don't miss out any steps – or make the gaps between them too big – or you might lose your reader.

For now, though, consider this: It took five chapters to detail the news writing style, while the more fluid drop intro has been explained in one. This is not to undermine the drop intro, but it does underline the fact that this is something many of us do already without knowing it. Most people only need to refine their drop intros, whereas getting to grips with the news writing approach is something that needs to be actively learnt and practised.

Think about it

Look back at some of the things you've written or read lately. Can you identify any drop intros? Do they grab your attention? Are they too long?

Have a go!

1 Pick a story that interests you and then write a drop intro for it. Write as many as you like from different angles to practise the technique. Try varying the length of the drop as well.

2 Now that you've seen the two different approaches (news style and drop intro) and practised them, which do you prefer? Which did you find easier to do?

7 The 'big reveal'

So there you have it. On the one hand, we have the rigid, structurally sound, disciplined approach of news writing. On the other, we have the rather fluid, creative approach of the drop intro. As individual approaches to writing, both have their merits and pitfalls. Knowing the pros and cons of both is key to embarking on any piece of writing. To me, these two approaches to writing sit at either ends of a broad spectrum and we can use them as two distinct techniques. However, we can also fuse them to create something uniquely different. And that's the beauty of writing this way. There are an infinite number of permutations where the two techniques can be interwoven and transformed to create the right approach for every piece of writing. Those who have never used the news writing style before have, in effect, been writing with one hand tied behind their back. And yet, the remedy is so straightforward.

For example, remember the story of the young tearaway who is trying to raise money for charity after he smashed up a stolen vehicle? Here are three different versions of the same story.

News writing style

An 18-year-old convicted car thief is planning to raise £250,000 for charity after he was involved in a near-fatal crash at a well-known accident blackspot.

One-sentence (eight words) drop intro

He was just a tearaway looking for kicks.
But when Jack Butler nearly died after stealing a car, he decided to make amends and raise £250,000 to pay his debt to society.

Six-sentence (72 words) drop intro:

The first thing he remembered was lying upside down in someone else's car. In the quiet of the night, all he heard was the trickle of a nearby stream. Then came the crackle of a small fire. When the smell of petrol fumes hit him he began to panic. The next thing he remembered was waking up in hospital, wincing in pain. For Jack Butler, this had been a very lucky escape. **That's because ...**

All three of these intros are about the same story. All three are perfectly acceptable. And yet, all three are quite different. So, which is the best one?

The answer depends on your answer to four simple questions:

Why are you writing?
What do you want to say?
Who is your audience?
How are you going to say it?

Once you know the answer to these questions, you can begin. And it's the same for all pieces of writing.

The four key questions

1 Why are you writing?

It might seem obvious, but before embarking on any piece of writing it's important to know why you're doing it. What's the purpose of this particular task? Do you want to relay some important information, such as the time and place for a meeting? Or is it something more subtle than that? Perhaps you want to influence your readers, make them buy a product or impress your tutor with your grasp of 18th-century politics?

Different reasons for writing dictate different approaches. For instance, if you were sending an email warning people about a cancelled event, would you use a meandering drop intro followed by 500 words of description, or would you use a punchy news style approach? If you know people are pushed for time, would you bury important information or highlight it for all to see?

2 What do you want to say?

Once again, this is a really simple question, but unless you know what you want to say, how can you sit down and write? However, by using the WWWWWH approach, you'll start to find answers. That's because it helps to marshal your thoughts and provides order in a chaos of ideas. Only by finding this order can you realistically attempt to write.

3 Who is your audience?

If you're a regular writer for a newspaper or magazine, you get a feel for your readership. In fact, the two-way conversation you have with them can be quite rewarding for a journalist on the lookout for new stories. If you don't work for a publication, it's still worth trying to figure out your audience. For instance, how much do they know about the subject you're writing about? If your topic is the launch of a new smartphone app, for example, does your target audience know the difference between the two main mobile operating systems, iOS and Android? Are they comfortable with jargon or do you have to explain things?

Once again, thinking about your readers helps to guide you as a writer and allows you to decide what kind of language you can use.

4 How are you going to say it?

The answer to this question depends on your replies to the previous three. Are you going to hit your reader between the eyes with a punchy news writing intro, or take a more softly softly approach with a drop intro? As before, the best way to explain how the different approaches work is to see them in action.

The four key questions – for a journalist

Reporter Danny Green at *The Daily Grind* has been given this story to follow up:

- The government has launched another PR initiative to get companies to reduce their carbon footprint.
- It's warning that a hike in energy bills – due to an increase in government-backed green taxes and the wholesale cost of energy – is inevitable.
- It's warning that companies can expect to see the cost of their energy bills rise significantly unless they take action now to mitigate the rising costs.

As a seasoned news reporter, Danny is pretty clear about his approach to the story.

Danny, why are you writing?

This is a cracking story that is definitely on *The Daily Grind*'s editorial radar. The paper's position is quite clear. With the mood in the country at the moment, we're pretty much against the government and its insistence on imposing ever-higher energy taxes. What's more, these higher taxes come at a time when the wholesale price of energy keeps on rising. Businesses are being hit with a double whammy of rising costs and increased taxes. It is simply not sustainable to keep asking businesses to pay more. That's why we'll run with this story – and I tell you what, the government is in for a hard time!

What do you want to say?

Pretty much what I've said already. Sorry, I got carried away a bit! To us, this story is just another example of the government's ludicrous energy policy. They've gone so far down the green agenda that they are threatening the fuel safety of the UK. If it goes on like this, we fear that companies will have to cut costs elsewhere – and that could mean jobs – just to keep the lights on. Or worse!

Who's your audience?

Our readership is just as sceptical as we are. They're opposed to windfarms that don't work when there's no wind or when it's blowing a gale. And they've had enough of paying subsidies for things that don't work. Ultimately, they're sick and tired of seeing their energy bills soar.

How are you going to say it?

I'm going to hit them between the eyes with a news story that will leave the government and our readers in no doubt about our thoughts on this matter. We're not pulling any punches. Heck, we might even fly a kite and warn people that they could be facing blackouts this winter.

As a result of this approach, Danny wrote the following:

> *The government has launched yet another energy initiative that does little to help UK plc cope with a sharp rise in fuel bills. It's warning companies that unless they start saving energy, there are real concerns that the lights could go out this winter.*
>
> *In a throwback to the 1970s, it seems the working week could be shortened to protect limited energy stocks.*

The four key questions – for a corporate manager

But Danny isn't the only one who has been eyeing this story. Over at the corporate headquarters of Shiretown Bank, Patrick Martin is part of the company's Corporate Social Responsibility team. CSR is a big feature at the bank. Shiretown's CSR team works to maintain and protect the image and brand of the bank. And being a responsible, sustainable business is part of that brand.

Patrick, why are you writing?

We've got more than 650 buildings across the UK, including bank branches, offices and computer datacentres. Our energy bill for last year was almost £30 million and we've pledged to reduce this figure year-on-year. But we can only do it with the help of our employees. We've been engaged in a long-running campaign to get them to think about energy use in our offices and branches. So, as part of our ongoing push towards greater energy efficiency, we can piggyback on the government's announcement to help reinforce the message to our staff.

What do you want to say?

I want to say that our staff need to re-double their efforts to save energy. That means switching off lights and computers when not in use. I know, I know … we've said this a dozen times before, but we need to keep on saying it and reminding people.

Who's your audience?

Actually, I've got two audiences. The first is an internal one – our employees. I'm going to put this in an email/memo from the director of CSR, talk about the government's latest initiative blah blah, and use it to remind everyone to think green.

But there's an external audience as well. Our CSR messaging is a great way for us to show our customers and other stakeholders that we are doing everything we can to help reduce our carbon footprint. They love that! It's very 'in vogue' at the moment.

So, I think this story could act as a springboard to discuss our green credentials. I'm thinking this could make a great blog from our CEO on our corporate website.

How are you going to say it?

Well, for the employee email I'm going to do a newsy drop intro and use some of the facts included in the government announcement. I might even use a quote from the Minister to give it some gravity. But I think I'll use a longer, softer drop for the CEO's blog targeting our external audience.

That way, it gives me room to make the case for being a green company, part of the global village, etc.

As a result of this approach, Patrick wrote the following:

Email to staff

As you may have heard in the news, the government is calling on companies such as ours to do more to save energy. For us at Shiretown Bank, reducing our carbon footprint is nothing new. Thanks to your help, we've already saved £3.5 million from our energy bill. But we can always do more. That's why I'm asking you to redouble your efforts ...

CEO blog

Here at Shiretown Bank, we know that running a profitable business is not enough. In today's world, we also have to run a good business. And by good, I mean ethical. That's why we spent more than £3 million last year on projects helping disadvantaged children in our inner cities. Our 'Time to Shine' initiative has brought hope to hundreds of young people, ensuring that they have a bright future.

Speaking of bright futures, we're in the middle of a seven-year initiative to reduce our carbon footprint and cut our energy use, while investing in sustainable green power. It's something we're embedding in every part of our business.

This is why I welcome the government's latest plans to get UK plc to focus on cutting its energy use. After all, reducing energy use doesn't just save money, it cuts carbon emissions and that's good for everyone.

Patrick knows that his drop intro for the CEO's blog is somewhat circuitous. It is more than 100 words before he gets to the government's energy saving initiative, and he realises it may also be a tad long. But Patrick isn't writing for himself. He's writing on behalf of the CEO and he knows that his boss likes to grandstand. Patrick has learnt that if he doesn't pander to his CEO's ego, the result can be much, much worse. So, he has to weigh things up very carefully to get the blog through the approvals process.

The four key questions – for a small business owner

North of the border in Glasgow, Sally Malone, head of a small consultancy firm specialising in tourism and recreation, has also seen the news. As the boss of a small firm, her focus for the last four years has been on growing the business and meeting the needs of her clients. But now that the firm is established, she's able to look at other areas that could help her business grow. And this government announcement has struck a chord.

Sally, why are you writing?

I had a meeting with our accountant last week and one of the things he highlighted was the double-digit increase in our energy bills. At the time, I thought there was nothing I could do about it. It's just one of those things. But having read this story from the government, it makes sense to me to look at ways in which we could reduce costs. After all, as a small business, we need to do everything we can to stay competitive in an ever-changing world. Too many companies have gone to the wall, and I am determined that we are not going to be one of them.

What do you want to say?

I don't know really. But what I want to do is kick-start a discussion with my team. I'm very inclusive like that. They're good with ideas – very creative – so I reckon that's where I should start.

Who's your audience?

My staff. They're a lovely bunch of people and I know this is something that will interest them as much as me.

How are you going to say it?

It's going to be a drop intro and I'm going to ask for their help. But I'm going to be informal.

As a result of weighing up her options, Sally decided to write the following:

Email to staff

I need your help! I want to have a meeting on Thursday to discuss ways we can help cut our energy use. Firstly, it could save us money and secondly, it will also help us to cut our carbon emissions. And I like the idea of that. In fact, we might be able to brainstorm a few ideas about some other green initiatives. I know you bright sparks will have plenty of ideas, so put your thinking caps on. Nothing is off limits, and I'll buy the doughnuts!

Sally

There you have it – one story and yet three completely different treatments, depending on the audience and reason for writing. By being methodical and asking the right questions, it's easy to see how you can tailor a piece of writing according to the needs of the audience. Patrick Martin – who knew that his CEO was a bit of a peacock – had an additional element to consider before undertaking the blog.

As these examples show, just about every piece of writing can be labelled as news writing style, drop or a fusion of the two. As I have pointed out, deciding which one to use depends on your reason for writing and your audience. This isn't just the case for stories written by journalists. It is equally true of everyday things that people have to write: emails, reports, blogs, web copy – you name it. News writing and feature writing may have their roots firmly planted in journalism, but that doesn't stop these techniques being used elsewhere. In the next chapter we will examine other types of writing and see how the principles we have discussed can be applied there.

Think about it

Look at some of the things you've written lately. In light of what you now know, what changes would you make to improve them?

Have a go!

Before you start your next piece of writing, answer the four key questions in this chapter and write down your answers. Use these answers to help you decide which approach will be most appropriate.

8 Writing beyond the newsroom

Up until now, most of the focus of this book has been on how journalistic techniques are used to write news stories and feature articles. Now, though, it's time to see these techniques move out of the newsroom and into the classroom ... the office ... the maintenance depot ... the hospital administrative centre.

And that's because I believe these skills and techniques are transferable. They can be exported out of the newsroom and into any educational or workplace setting. The difference, of course, is that if you work for a car dealership, an insurance company or an international mining corporation, the chances are you won't be writing 'stories' as such. Instead, written work is more likely to involve emails, letters and reports. However, it may help if you view whatever you are writing as 'a story' because the principles are the same.

Once you've learnt the basic techniques, the skill lies in seeing how you can adapt them for your particular situation. One thing is certain: it doesn't take long to see these techniques in action in the 'real world'.

The company memo

As you all know, earlier this year we launched our new range of wines packaged in eco-friendly plastic wine bottles. The response from our customers has been above expectations, and we've seen sales of these wines increase 17% in just a few months.

The use of these lighter bottles has already helped us save more than 20,000 tonnes of carbon dioxide. And since the wine is now bottled in the UK rather than in Chile, this has led to significant cost savings in shipping.

Working with our partners in other wine-producing regions of the world, we're now in the process of expanding the range of wines we produce in plastic bottles. We're even running tests that involve putting some sparkling wines in recyclable aluminium cans.

As a result, we now plan to expand our bottling plant in Cardiff with a £7.5m investment plan over three years. This will secure 35 existing jobs and create a further 30 positions. Further details of these plans will be released later next month.

What fantastic news! The introduction of the new plastic wine bottles has been a roaring success. But unfortunately, by using a drop intro that spans three paragraphs and 120 words, the CEO has buried the good news about the jobs at the bottom.

You'll also notice that this memo is structured according to the chronology of events rather than the importance of the information. This chronological way of writing is commonly used by people who haven't been trained in news writing. And yet, with a small number of changes you could have this, which is far more compelling:

To: All staff

From: The CEO

Re: 30 new jobs to be created thanks to success of plastic wine bottles

I am pleased to report that thanks to the roaring success of our plastic wine bottles, we plan to invest £7.5m in our bottling plant in Cardiff. Not only will this secure 35 existing jobs at the site, it will also create a further 30 more positions.

This is excellent news. As you all know, earlier this year we launched our new range of wines packaged in eco-friendly plastic wine bottles. The response from our customers has been above expectations, and we've seen sales of these wines increase 17% in just a few months.

The use of these lighter bottles has already helped us save more than 20,000 tonnes of carbon dioxide. And since the wine is now bottled in the UK rather than in Chile, this has led to significant cost savings in shipping.

Working with our partners in other wine-producing regions of the world, we're in the process of expanding the range of wines we produce in plastic bottles. We're even running tests that involve putting some sparkling wines in recyclable aluminium cans.

I want to finish by congratulating you all on an excellent year's work. These are exciting times, and I look forward to sharing further details of the plans with you all later next month.

By making minimal – but essential – changes to the structure, the whole tone of the memo is transformed from rather uninspiring to celebratory. Indeed, staff at the company might even be allowed to open a can or two of fizz to celebrate! The information supporting the decision to expand – the success of the plastic bottle initiative – is relevant, so there's no need to edit this out, but it doesn't need to go first.

To someone trained in the news writing technique, it's such an obvious thing to do. And yet the difference is marked. If you're in any doubt, show these two memos to someone who hasn't read this book. Ask them which they prefer and why? In fact, feel free to poll a number of colleagues to get a good spread of opinions. I believe the majority of them will prefer the second example for all the reasons set out in the book so far, but, in some cases, they won't necessarily know why. That is until you point it out to them.

In a sense, this example epitomises what this book is about. If you have any experience of the workplace, you will, no doubt, have had to read a company memo or notice. They're rarely exciting. Worthy is often the best that can be said of them. And yet, by thinking of the reader, it is possible to create something that is much more inspiring.

The email

The next example is an email that was sent out to guests, visitors and delegates attending a conference at a hotel. It's such a poor example it's difficult to know where to start. But, by being methodical, it's easy to see what needs to be done.

To: All guests, visitors and conference delegates

Subject: Hotel snow closure

Dear guests,

You will be aware that widespread snow is forecast for tomorrow, beginning roughly at the time the Future of Synthetic Sausage Skin Conference is due to start. The Met Office has issued a yellow warning for snow for this area.

As you know, here at the Briarside Hotel we enjoy a wonderful rural location, high on the North Hills. Because of the nature of our site, we know that everybody has a potentially challenging journey to our hotel when roads may be unsafe due to snow or ice. Many of our visitors and staff live in country areas and travel long distances to come to our hotel. At this moment, there is serious doubt as to whether public transport will be operating. I hope you understand that planning for the safe journeys of our guests and our staff when heavy snowfall is forecast is a most important aspect of our decision-making.

I have been reviewing the conditions with my management team today and I've also spoken to those in charge of public transport in the area. The safety of the site and safe access to and from the site is our main priority for all hotel guests, visitors and staff. Whilst I am currently delaying any final decision as to whether we will need to close the hotel and postpone the conference tomorrow — as we are all aware of the slightly unpredictable nature of weather and forecasting — there is a strong likelihood that we may need to shut on Wednesday 13th January for the whole day.

It is essential that all guests, visitors and conference delegates review the hotel website this evening after 6 pm for further updates or changes. I stress that the website and also email will be the forms of communication used to inform guests, visitors and conference delegates of any possible changes to our normal opening schedule and operating procedures, rather than the telephone.

I thank you for your understanding in advance and will email you early this evening.

Yours sincerely

B Soames

Hotel Manager

What is the 'story'?

Snow is forecast which could shut the hotel. A decision on whether it will be shut will be posted on the hotel website from 6 pm this evening. That's all!

Is this news writing style or a drop intro?

It is a drop intro. A very long one – almost 300 words. In fact, the length is so extreme and the content so absurd that the result is comical. And yet, emails and letters such as this are all too common.

Is all the information contained in this email relevant?

In the circumstances, do we really need to be reminded that the hotel 'enjoys a wonderful rural location, high on the North Hills'? Do we need to know the different transport arrangements of hotel visitors and staff or about the health and safety 'box ticking' being carried out by the hotel's senior management team?

Not only is this email structurally unsound, the content is wayward as well. Here are a couple of ways it could be improved:

> *Because of the threat of heavy snow, I am writing to inform you that we will make a decision later this afternoon as to whether we will be forced to shut the hotel tomorrow and postpone the conference. We will publish our decision on the hotel website by 6 pm this evening.*
>
> *Yours sincerely*

Or:

> *I am writing to warn you that tomorrow's conference may be postponed because of the forecast of heavy snow. A decision will be made this afternoon and published on our website by 6 pm this evening.*

Neither of these alternatives is going to win any prizes for creative writing. But they do, at least, distil what needs to be said – a massive improvement on what was originally sent out.

The letter

Here's another example that's worth looking at. It's from a telephone utility company, warning customers that their service could be disrupted because of planned maintenance work.

Dear customer

During the week commencing 27 June, UK Phoneco will be carrying out essential maintenance work in your area to upgrade the phone and broadband network. This is part of a nationwide project to bring our network into the 21st century. It is possible that you will suffer some disruption to your phone and internet service during this time.

Any interruption to your service will only last up to 30 minutes at the longest. However, if you are without phone and internet service for more than ONE HOUR, please call the special helpline printed at the bottom of this letter.

Over the last five years, UK Phoneco has invested some £5 billion in upgrading the phone and broadband network across the UK. It is part of our investment in the UK and has full backing from the government.

The rest of the letter goes on to discuss the benefits of an upgraded phone network and the things it allows homes and businesses to do.

What is the 'story'?

UK Phoneco is due to carry out essential maintenance work in your area and they are writing to let you know that your phone and internet connection may be lost for a while.

Is it a new style intro or a drop intro?

It's a news style approach with a slight twist. The first sentence tells you the *when, who, what* and *where*. The second tells you *why* the work is being carried out, and the third tells you that you may suffer some disruption (*what*). Arguably, though, it is the fourth sentence that is most important, because it explains what you should do if you lose your phone and internet connection for more than an hour. However, it would be difficult to place this information any higher in the letter because the context – maintenance work may cause disruption – has to come first, otherwise it is meaningless.

What this shows is that using journalistic writing techniques isn't always plain sailing. At times, it can be cumbersome and tricky. Which is why there has to be scope to bend or break the rules.

The press release

It doesn't matter whether it is an important government announcement or publicity for a village play, the structure of a press release should be similar to that of a news story. That's because most press releases mirror the news writing style by putting the most important information first. Take a look at this example from an anti-bankers pressure group:

> *June 27, London. Go Bankers! – the pressure group that speaks out against the excesses of the financial world – says the decision to hand out free £10 notes by Shiretown Bank is little more than 'a gimmick'. Instead of wasting time on PR stunts, the bank should start lending to businesses that need the money.*
>
> *Go Bankers! spokeswoman Erica Jones said: 'Shiretown Bank is a disgrace. If its chief exec thinks that standing on the steps of the Bank of England handing out money will appease his critics, he is wrong.*
>
> *'I urge members of the public not to accept this money, regardless of how tempting it might be. Instead, they should refuse. He'd look a proper Charlie if he couldn't even give the stuff away.'*

Like many press releases, this example follows the shape and form of the inverted news writing triangle. However, I think the author of this particular press release has missed a trick. Yes, it follows the rules of news writing and yes, it has something interesting to say which is likely to be picked up by the press.

But what about coming at this from a different angle? What about making the protest – the refusal to accept the money – the most important part of the story?

June 27, London. Go Bankers! – the pressure group that speaks out against the excesses of the financial world – has called on the public to show their dissatisfaction with the banks by refusing to accept free £10 notes due to be handed out by the Shiretown Bank boss tomorrow.

In a stand of defiance, the pressure group is urging people to refuse the handout, which it claims is little more than 'a gimmick'.

Go Bankers! spokeswoman Erica Jones said: 'Shiretown Bank is a disgrace. If its chief exec thinks standing on the steps of the Bank of England handing out money will appease his critics, he is wrong.

'I urge members of the public not to accept this money regardless of how tempting it might be. Instead, they should refuse. He'd look a proper Charlie if he couldn't even give the stuff away.

'Instead of wasting time on PR stunts, the bank should start lending to businesses that need the money.'

Like the previous example, this press release is based on the news writing principles, but with a difference: the angle is more left field. By simply changing the order, we've changed the emphasis. It's only a subtle change, but it's a much better angle, and this has nothing to do with creative writing. Instead, it's all about creative thinking.

Of course, there are times when people don't use the news writing technique for press releases, but use a drop intro, which is more characteristic of feature writing:

Cambridge, June 12: It's been the coldest spring on record. But thankfully, the last week has seen the UK basking in temperatures above 20°C. With the risk of frosts now well behind us, it's time for gardeners to consider their summer bedding plants.

At the Salsify Nursery in Cambridge, we've been ensuring that our bedding plants are in tip-top form for the summer. As professional nurserymen, we've ensured that our plants have remained undercover and stress-free, protected from the cold temperatures and harsh winds.

As a result, our bedding plants are bigger and stronger than you might find at a gardening superstore. And bigger and stronger plants mean loads more flowers until the first frost ...

Here, the drop intro is used and is perfectly acceptable for a business that doesn't want to rush in with, in effect, 'now that the frosts have gone, come and buy our summer bedding plants'. Instead, the drop intro here softens that rather abrupt message to something that is more agreeable. Again, this shows the versatility of using journalistic techniques in everyday settings.

The blog

Self-publishing has become big business. Blogging – whether for business or pleasure – gives people a chance to write about whatever they like and reach out to a worldwide audience. Some people describe blogs as being like entries in a diary or journal.

That may be true, but the principles of good writing remain the same. Here's an entry from someone who writes a regular blog about life in Yorkshire.

Last week, I visited the lovely village of Hawes in the Yorkshire Dales. It's a beautiful village with cobbled streets, traditional shops and a river that you can stare at for hours. Which is what I was doing when a young man came and sat down beside me. We got chatting and it emerged that he was walking from John O'Groats to Land's End.

It's great to see young people take on such challenges, but he then explained that he was doing it for charity. He wanted to raise an astonishing £250,000 for the emergency services because they had helped save his life after a car crash. I was already enthralled by his adventure when he candidly told me that he had caused the crash after he'd stolen the car, and that after a long stay in hospital, he had been sent to prison for his crime.

I was so astonished by the encounter that I gave him £5 towards his fundraising. He thanked me and then, after a drink of water, went on his way. As I watched him stride up the cobbled road, I couldn't help but think of

*what had just happened. Part of me wanted
to pat this young man on the back for
turning his life around. Another part thought
I'd just been hoodwinked.*

In case you haven't already worked it out, the first
paragraph of the blog entry is a drop intro, and the
nub of the story is teased out in 80 words or so in
the second paragraph. Of course, it could have been
done in fewer words. But that would have removed
much of its charm. This is a personal blog, and the
writer is perhaps more interested in writing for
themselves than in attracting a large number of
readers. So, in this instance – where there is
nothing at stake aside from a curious anecdote – the
writer is perfectly free to take their time.

As you can see, different writing tasks can all benefit from an understanding of news writing, the drop intro and the other techniques highlighted throughout this book. These journalistic techniques have a part to play in all types of writing, and anyone who chooses to adopt them will see their writing improve. But what if you are still unhappy with your writing development?

Think about it

The premise of this book is that tried and tested journalistic techniques can be transposed from the newsroom to the workplace, the classroom, the HR office, the government department, the charity, etc. Have a look at the written work your organisation produces and see if it matches what you've learnt so far. And based on what you know now, how could you improve it?

9 Refining your writing

If you have understood and followed the advice so far, the chances are that you'll be starting to produce some pretty good pieces of writing. The more you write, the better you will become. And before you know it, writing this way will become second nature. Indeed, you'll begin to understand that learning the news writing technique – and developing it for your own needs, as highlighted in the previous chapter – is a great way to build on the skills you already have.

It will take you to a new level of ability, which will ensure you maximise your chances of being read. But as valuable as these techniques are, this isn't the end of the process. For as any student of writing knows, there is always something new to learn. From drafting and reviewing to proofing and editing, there are many tasks you have to perform as a writer. In fact, there are a gazillion things we could talk about – including the use of hyperbole. Instead, I've listed the top five points that repeatedly crop up when I talk to teachers, editors and others who regularly read other people's work. It may not be an exhaustive list, but it includes some of the most common issues facing all of us.

1 Sentence wordcount

If there is one thing you could do today to improve your writing it is this: as a general rule of thumb, aim for around 20 words per sentence. Now, that number is not fixed in stone. Neither is it some arbitrary figure I've plucked out of the air. Instead, it's based on the development of journalism over the years and the way that writing has evolved. Let me explain. When I was a young student of journalism, I was told that the average wordcount for the tabloid press was around 12 to 14 words per sentence. At the other end of the scale, the broadsheet newspapers would average in excess of 30 words a sentence. The mid-market papers tended to have average sentence wordcounts somewhere in the middle.

Fast-forward to today, and the average tabloid sentence wordcount is nudging a little higher at around 15 or 16 words a sentence, while most broadsheets have, on the whole, managed to make it under 30 words. Once again, the mid-market papers continue to hold the middle ground. Now, I'm the first to hold up my hand and admit that this isn't based on some scientific study where every single word ever produced has been counted and filed away in a big computer. No, it's merely an observation that anyone can make if they are prepared to count the number of words in sentences from different publications. However, if you did, you would see that there is a movement towards the middle ground – around 20 words a sentence – which provides a useful guide. So what has this to do with writing a brochure for a bank, an advert for a car dealership or a website for a guesthouse?

The truth is, if you regularly write sentences with wordcounts that are in the high 20s or break the 30-word barrier, you need to start reining back. Why? Because the longer the sentence, the more chance you have of making it difficult to read. Also, the longer the sentence, the greater the danger that you will make a grammatical faux pas. And that could be a real turn-off for your readers. Equally, you need to ensure that your sentences aren't so short that they disrupt the flow of your text.

Does this mean all your sentences need to be exactly 20 words? No, of course not! It's merely a guide. But it is a way for you to analyse your own writing and that of others. And it's one that works and is guaranteed to deliver results.

If you're unconvinced about the role that sentence length plays, check this out. It's best if you read it aloud:

> *Short sentences give emphasis. They pack a punch. The shorter they are, the harder they hit. There's more action. More pizzazz. Short sentences provide impact. They spit at you. OK? Too many short sentences sound like bullet points. So use them sparingly. Got that?*

Although short sentences do pack a punch, too many can make the text sound abrupt. Take this news story, for example:

> *A new shop has opened in the High Street. It specialises in selling old vinyl records. The owner used to work in the City. He decided to open the shop as people have turned their backs on digital downloads.*

This intro – written in a news writing style – contains all the relevant information. But it doesn't read well because the sentences are too short. Thankfully, remedying this isn't too taxing:

> *A new music shop has opened in the High Street, specialising in buying and selling old vinyl records. The owner – who gave up his job in the City to open the store – embarked on his new venture when he realised people were turning their backs on digital downloads.*

If you read both examples – especially if you read them out aloud – you should be able to hear the difference. The first stops and starts, whereas the second has a pleasing pace and tone.

Then again, there is the issue of long sentences:

> *Sentences which are too long, however, have the opposite effect and tend to slow down the pace of a piece of writing, and, as such, are generally more useful for making statements or commenting on things in a calm and more reasoned manner that requires thought, consideration and perhaps a smidgen of self-analysis. They can prove to be a perfect antidote to short sentences. Sometimes, you'll see a long sentence immediately adjacent to a short one and they work. Why? Because when you add the wordcounts together and divide by the number of*

*sentences, it gets somewhere near that
magic '20 is plenty'. One of the problems
with really long sentences is that they can be
unwieldy and difficult to keep under control
– much like a disobedient Jack Russell on
the end of a long leash that has been
distracted by a rat or young rabbit and is
intent on flushing out its prey with complete
disregard for its owner.*

Once again, if you read the text above out loud,
you should be able to hear the effects of using long
and short sentences and a mixture of the two.
Here's an example of a particularly long sentence:

*In light of research published today by the
government, which suggests that more and
more people are working from home instead
of commuting, a company in Rotherham has
unveiled plans for a new digital tagging
system that allows workers to 'clock in' and
'clock out' as if they had attended work in
person.*

This sentence reads well, but at over 50 words, it is
simply too long. And yet, with some nimble editing
it can easily be cut to a better length:

*A Rotherham firm has unveiled plans for a
new system that allows home workers to
'clock in' and 'clock out' as if they had*

attended work in person. The announcement follows the publication of research by the government, which suggests that more and more people are working from home instead of commuting.

There are no hard and fast rules about sentence wordcount – just guidance based on experience. By pivoting around the 20-word sentence limit, you won't go far astray. But, of course, if every sentence hovers around this 20-word limit your writing will lack variety. It will become monotonous. By using a combination of long and short sentences – along with your 20-word norm – you will help maintain your reader's interest.

2 Draft and re-draft

It doesn't matter whether you're a novice or a professional, everyone – without exception – should review their writing. It's common sense really. And yet you'd be surprised how many students – and how many people in the workplace – write something and send it straight off without giving it a second thought. In fact, speaking to business managers and teachers, I find that this is one of their biggest bugbears: people simply do not review their written work. And yet, drafting and redrafting is important in so many ways.

If you think about it logically, the drafting process ensures:

- that you've said what you want to say and that your message is crystal clear;
- that you've written for your intended audience in language that is suitable for them;
- that you've used all your best words, phrases and angles;
- that the structure of your writing is sound, ensuring maximum readership;
- that you've achieved a high level of grammatical and spelling accuracy.

I'll be honest, drafting and redrafting can, at times, be difficult. It can be tedious. It can be a real slog. Which is why there is no easy way to say this: no matter how difficult you find it, redrafting and reviewing your work is something that should become embedded into your everyday writing routine. There is no magic bullet for this task, except one tip I have for you, and that is always to read your piece of text aloud. Here's why:

It will make sure it sounds right

You'll find that hearing your writing allows you to judge whether sentences are too long (because you'll be needing to take breaths), too short (because the sentences will sound abrupt or like a series of bullet points) or just right (with a pleasing timbre). Also, if you trip over words while you speak, it's highly likely that your readers will stumble, too. If that happens, a simple correction – such as breaking a long sentence into two or using a synonym or paraphrase – will help the flow.

It will help to eradicate repetition of words and phrases because repetition of words and phrases can be annoying to the reader

We've all done it – used the same word over and over in the same sentence, paragraph or page. It's not one of the worst crimes ever committed but, all the same, it's a stylistic error that can be very easily resolved. One editor I know says that the repetition of words is the most common stylistic error that she sees when work is submitted to her. In most cases, it is people who have not reviewed their work who are most likely to be guilty of this, but even people who do check their work may not spot repetitions. Reading your words aloud increases the chances that you will notice any repetitions and correct them where necessary.

It will improve your accuracy

Checking your writing and working through the drafting process helps you spot those typos, boo-boos, shockers or just plain old mistakes that can sully a piece of writing. Whether caused by an innocent slip of a finger or the result of a grammatical blind spot, these errors can be a byword for sloppy unprofessionalism and a symptom of undue care and attention. If you're in any doubt, here's a question for you. Would you trust a firm that advertised *All You're Stationary Needs* to print your wedding invitations or the order of service for your best friend's funeral? Thought not.

There are loads of brilliant resources, both online and offline, that can help you improve your accuracy, including your computer's spell checker (see below). Which you decide to use is up to you. Just remember that, as with the news style writing technique, written accuracy is something you have to work at. It requires concentration and hard work. But, as with many things in life, the more you work at it, the easier it gets.

3 The computer spelling and grammar checker

Too many people rely on computer spelling and grammar checkers without realising that they aren't always right. Some teachers report that this is a particular issue with young people. While spell checkers have come on by leaps and bounds since the advent of the first word processors, they are still not infallible. When it comes to using a spell checker, there are three rules you need to follow:

- First, make sure it is working in the right language. You'd be amazed how many people have it unknowingly set to US English – often by default – when they are using UK English, for example, or vice versa. That doesn't just happen in the classroom, but in the workplace as well.

- Second, don't believe everything it tells you. Be sceptical. Try to figure out why it's making a suggestion. Only when you are happy that it's correct should you accept the change it is suggesting.
- Finally, use it as a learning tool to improve your grammar and spelling. Question and analyse the suggestions it makes and, when you agree that it has identified an error in your writing, take note of this and try to ensure you don't make that mistake in future.

4 Identify an expert/mentor

If you work in a company or organisation, make the most of those around you in your own department or elsewhere. Identify an expert or, better still, ask for a mentor to help you improve your accuracy and writing skills. By tapping into someone else's knowledge, you can learn a great deal about the subtleties and variations of writing. A mentor can show you where you are going wrong and what you are getting right, and a good mentor at any stage in your career – whether in education or the workplace – will prove invaluable. After all, it's exactly the same process used by newspaper and magazine editors to train young writers. However, don't expect a mentor to drop everything just to look at your work – after all, they're busy people with their own jobs to do, and they're doing you a favour. That said, no one usually minds being interrupted if you accompany your request for help with a cup of tea and their favourite biscuit!

5 Use a style guide

Whatever organisation you write for, you should be able to lay your hands on an in-house style guide. This outlines a standardised approach to how things should be written and, if used properly, it helps to ensure consistency across an entire organisation, regardless of size. The style guide is the arbiter on issues such as alternative spellings, for example realise or realize. It also helps provide consistency for the spelling of new words and acronyms. For example, it will establish the acceptable way to spell the shortened version of *wireless internet broadband – WiFi, wifi, Wifi, Wi-Fi* or *WI-FI*, or a company's new product – is it the *i-widget, I-Widget, i-Widget* or *iwidget*?

A style guide can be a single page document or it can be the length of a novel. Regardless of length, the most important thing about it is that it should be used and updated when needed. It is not a document to be filed away or left on a shelf gathering dust. The widespread use of a style guide is a sign that your company or organisation takes writing seriously. Like the news writing technique, it's a form of discipline and structure that contributes to greater clarity, understanding and professionalism.

✳ ✳ ✳

This book is all about using tools and techniques to maximise your chances of being read, regardless of what it is you are writing. By thinking about WWWWWH, angle, structure and the words that are available to you before you start writing, you can expect to see improvements. By employing the news writing technique, your writing will be better, more interesting and more accurate. You'll be able to write faster and with more skill and finesse. By knowing the rules – and how to break them – you will become a more accomplished writer. Above all, by thinking of your reader, not only will you improve your chances of being read, you will earn the right to be read.

ABOUT THE AUTHOR

Tim Richardson is a journalist who has been writing for more than 20 years. During a nine-year stint at *The Register* – the UK's best IT news website – he was the internet editor, writing hard-hitting stories and features on a daily basis. As a freelance journalist, he has also written for national newspapers and magazines, and spent a number of years as a Wimbledon tennis correspondent. Over the last decade or so, he has dedicated more and more of his time to training people to make the most of their communications skills. It was this passion to help others and to see them thrive that was the catalyst for writing this book.

Printed in Great Britain
by Amazon.co.uk, Ltd.,
Marston Gate.